Abbygale Sews

20 Simple Sewing Projects

For Eden, Izzy, Mum, Dad and, most of all, Marcus,
my love, my inspiration, my guiding light.

Beth

For Andy, Floyd, Sam & Summer.

Emma x

Emma Curtis
& Elizabeth Parnell

Abbygale Sews

20 Simple Sewing Projects

Search Press

Contents

Hello!

We are Emma and Beth, the creators of Abbygale Sews and two down-to-earth, everyday women with busy lives and families. We first met when working at a publishing company and quickly found that we shared a similar outlook on life, liked the same things and loved the vintage floral style. We are lucky enough to live in Devon, a beautiful part of England and these surroundings, along with our family and friends, inspired us to create the Abbygale style.

The story of Abbygale started when we fell pregnant at the same time and spent a good deal of our maternity leave together. With both of us being off work, money was tight, so at Christmas we decided to make all the presents ourselves! We made biscuits and cakes, chutneys and jams in decorated jars, children's sock monsters and fabric bags of all shapes and sizes. Our bags were well-made and stylish and were an instant success. Not long after that we created a brand name and labels for everything we made. We then started selling our bags on a market stall but finding it difficult to keep up with demand, we had the idea of producing them as kits. These contain everything you need to have a go, regardless of your level of skill or previous experience.

Now we find ourselves in the fantastic position of writing this book, so we can share some of our simple project ideas with an even wider audience. We want to inspire you to create something in our distinctive style where beauty doesn't have to be complicated! We feel there is a real place in society for lovingly crafted, handmade items. Our philosophy has always been, 'Why buy something manufactured when you can make your own unique items that fit your style precisely?'.

What level of experience is required?
No sewing experience is required to make any of the projects in this book, although a desire to craft is necessary.

We offer inspiration to those who own a sewing machine but have never dared use it and those who have bought craft kits in the past but never opened them. We've made this book uncomplicated and easy to follow so that you will succeed in every project you try. More experienced crafters will also benefit from these projects as there are plenty of opportunities to add your own creative twist to anything we do.

What equipment is required for the projects?
In short, just the basics! We always sew using a sewing machine although the smaller projects can be created by hand. When you start we recommend you have these items available:

- Dressmaker's pins and needles
- Sewing machine
- Iron
- Fabric marker/ dressmaker's chalk
- Stitch ripper
- Tape measure
- Safety pins
- A cup of tea and some biscuits!

Why you will love this book
This book presents each project with clear step-by-step instructions, all beautifully illustrated by Beth's husband Marcus. Each one is tried and tested, has a genuine story behind it and has been created with the love and care you will come to expect from Abbygale. All projects have been created in a way that allows you to personalise the end result easily, so however you choose to finish them, we know they will look amazing. You are, of course, free to use any fabric you like for the projects, but the fabrics featured throughout are all available from the Hamble & Jemima website www.hambleandjemima.co.uk and all Abbygale stockists. Needless to say, they are of excellent quality.

Emma   Beth

Gifts & Handmade Treasures

I certainly find giving gifts much more pleasurable than receiving them. It is such a great feeling to know that you have been able to make someone smile by giving them a thoughtful present. The only thing better than buying someone a gift is making one for them. Handmade gifts show that you have really spent the time (rather than money) thinking about the person you are making them for, and wrapping them in some brown paper and pretty ribbon will add that extra-special touch.

My family love the hampers I put together at Christmas, bursting with handmade treats, all wrapped and presented in lovely jars and bottles with home-made labels and paper tags. When Beth and I first started making things one Christmas, it was such a revelation. Our friends and families were absolutely thrilled to receive our handmade offerings so we have included a few of these great ideas in this chapter.

Our most popular handmade gift by far is the iconic Three-Way Sling Sac. This bag is still our most requested design from friends who regularly put in their orders around the time of their birthdays! I always encourage my friends to have a go themselves, as it's a simple design using just two pieces of fabric. The technique of sewing the right sides together and pulling through a gap in the fabric is so satisfying and always amazes me even after all this time!

The huggy doll project (page 16) is such a cute gift idea for children, as not only can you personalise it, you can also go to town on embellishments and even create a family of them for someone special.

Spread a little happiness!

Handy Pouch

This pouch is so easy to make and has endless uses: I use mine to keep all my cosmetics in, my eldest son uses his for storing his pens and pencils, my middle son stashes a handheld games console in his and my daughter has one too, in which she keeps a pair of princess shoes! I love the design – it reminds me of opening an envelope and it uses only small amounts of fabric (you can make four from 1 metre, or 1 yard, of fabric). Start making these handy pouches in the run-up to Christmas to give as gifts, or use as an extra-special gift bag with another present inside. It can be made to match other home-made bags, or try using PVC fabric to make it waterproof.

A truly versatile little bag!

Materials

35 x 44cm (13¾ x 17¼in) of outer fabric
35 x 50cm (13¾in x 19¾in) of lining fabric
1 button
45cm (17¾in) of ribbon

Step 1

Cut both the outer and lining fabrics in half. Both outer pieces should be 3cm (1¼in) shorter than the lining. Sew on a button about 9cm (3½in) from the bottom of one outer piece.

Step 2

Place the two pieces of outer fabric right sides together. Cut a 30cm (11¾in) length of the ribbon and fold it in half to make a loop. Sandwich this between the two pieces of outer fabric (as shown) before pinning and sewing down both sides and along the bottom, leaving the top, long edge open.

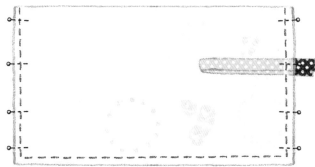

Step 3

Place the two pieces of lining fabric right sides together. Sew down both sides and along the bottom, leaving a 10cm (4in) gap in the centre for turning through later. Make sure that the seams match exactly on the outer and the lining fabric or the bag will not fit together properly.

Step 4

Tuck the outer fabric inside the lining so that the right sides are facing each other and the seams are aligned. Make sure that the top edges of both the lining and the outer fabric are flush with each other. Fold the remaining 15cm (6in) ribbon in half and tuck the looped end in between the two fabrics on the opposite side to the button. Leave about 1cm (½in) of ribbon poking out of the top, then carefully pin and sew the lining and the outer fabric together around the top edge as shown.

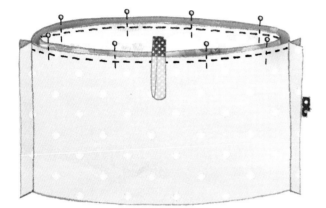

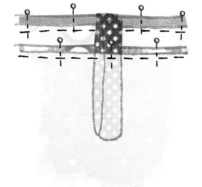

Step 5

Reach through the gap in the lining and pull the bag through so that it is the right way out. Tuck the lining inside the bag. Now tug the lining up to create a lip of fabric at the top of the bag, about 2.5cm (1in) deep. Iron this nice and flat and then sew around the top about 7mm (¼in) from the edge. The lining should now fit the insides and reach the bottom of the bag nicely.

Step 6

Fold over the top of the bag like an envelope so that the ribbon loop meets the button and iron this in place. Sew up the hole in the lining.

Step 7

Fill the pouch with goodies!

Three-Way
Sling Sac

With three young children and all the paraphernalia that comes with us wherever we go like wet wipes, endless snacks, random toys and spare clothes, it is most important that my 'everyday' bag is as practical as possible. The Three-Way Sling Sac is spot-on and is so versatile, I can wear it long across my body, adjust the poppers on the strap and carry it like a handbag, or knot the strap to a length of my choice. Of all the items people ask me to make for them, this is the most popular, so it would be a great gift for a friend or new mum.

You can literally sling it anywhere!

Materials

Template cut-outs for Three-Way Sling Sac
2 pieces 50 x 70cm (19¾ x 27 ½in) of outer fabric
2 pieces 50 x 70cm (19¾ x 27 ½in) of lining fabric
1 button
4 sets of poppers (press-studs)
20cm (7¾in) of ribbon

Step 1

Use the template provided to cut four pieces of fabric (two for the outside and two for the lining). Face the right sides of the outer fabric together, then pin and sew up the left and right edges. Repeat this process with the lining.

Step 2

Turn the outer fabric right side out and re-fold so that the seam you have just created runs centrally. Sew on the button.

Step 3

Turn the outer fabric inside-out again to match the lining. Re-fold each piece so that the seams are in the centre of the bag, then pin and sew along the bottom of each one. Be sure to leave a small gap of about 8cm (3¼in) in the lining for turning through later.

Step 4

Hand sew the 'male' poppers on to the right side of the lining and outer fabric as shown above. (Note: it's important to ensure that the positioning of the poppers is as accurate as possible as they must snap together when the bag is finished.) Sew the 'female' poppers on to the right side of the outer and lining fabric, aligning them with the corresponding 'male' poppers on the other side (shown above right).

Step 5

To create the bag's depth, take the outer part of the bag, turn inside out, pull out the bottom two corners, then sew across 4cm (1½in) from each corner point. Once sewn, trim off the triangles as shown and repeat this process with the lining.

Step 6

Tuck the lining inside the outer fabric, making sure that right sides are facing each other and that the centre seams line up. Fold the piece of ribbon in half and tuck this between the lining and the outer fabric on the opposite side to the button. Leave 1cm (½in) of ribbon poking out. Pin and sew around the top rim and handles of the bag.

Step 7

Unpin the bag and check that all the seams are closed, then locate the hole you left in the lining in Step 3. Reach through and carefully pull the whole bag inside out. The handle holes will be quite narrow, but will gradually pull through with a little patience. Push the lining back inside the bag before ironing it all nice and flat.

Step 8

Once all the edges are neat and flat, top stitch around the top rim of the bag on both sides, starting at the top of each handle. Try to stay as close to the edge as possible without straying off the fabric – take your time and the result will look really professional. Sew up the hole in the lining.

My Huggy Doll

Each birthday I try to make my girls something original, and I have quite a bit of fun thinking up quirky little projects to make them smile. This year was no exception when I spent a couple of evenings creating these little huggy dolls for their beds. I love using inkjet fabric paper when creating; it opens up a whole world of crafty possibilities for personalised presents. This little project is great for using scraps of fabrics as well as any odd little buttons and embellishments you have lying around... Let your favourite family photos be your inspiration and create some cute little dolls of your own!

Smiley happy people!

Step 1

From the template provided cut out the two body parts and one bib from the co-ordinating fabrics. Place the bib on top of the main body fabric, tack and then sew in place on the very edges of the bib fabric. Remove the tacking stitches.

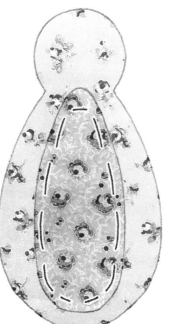

Materials

Template cut-outs for Huggy Dolls
2 pieces 35 x 25cm (13¾ x 9¾in) of fabric for doll
15 x 20cm (6 x 7¾in) of fabric for bib
1 sheet of inkjet fabric paper
Photographs of children's faces about 10cm
 (4in) diameter
50cm (19¾in) of ric-rac or other trimming
2 self-covered or decorative buttons (any size)
1 zip about 23cm (9in) long (optional)
Wadding
50cm (19¾in) of ribbon or lace trim

Step 2

Pin the decorative trimming around the edge of the bib then sew it in place.

Step 3

Using an inkjet printer, print out some faces on to the inkjet fabric paper. (We have used our children's faces, about 10cm (4in) in diameter). Cut out a face (you can add a border if you like) and peel off the backing paper. Tack the face in place, slightly overlapping the bib and trimming. Leave a small gap and push through a small handful of the wadding. Fix into place with a zigzag stitch around the whole face. Remove the tacking stitches.

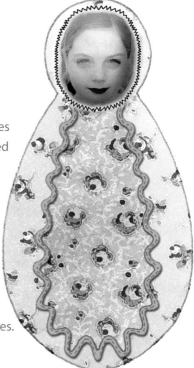

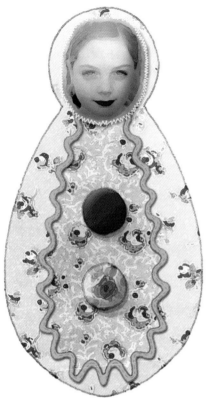

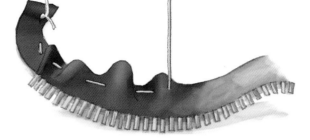

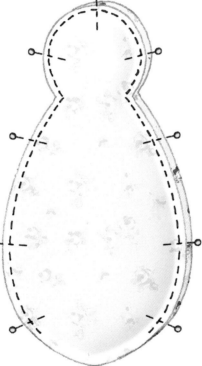

Step 4

Sew the self-covered or decorative buttons centrally on to the bib.

Step 5

Pin the dolly right sides together. Sew together with a 1cm (½in) seam, leaving a gap at the bottom. Turn the dolly out.

Step 6

Fill with wadding and sew the bottom seam closed by hand.

Step 7

To make a zip corsage, snip the bottom end off the zip and remove the zipper pull. Sew a large running stitch along the fabric edge on the opposite side from the teeth. Pull and gather your thread, then adjust until you are pleased with the shape. Sew to fix the shape and stitch on to your doll.

Step 8

Tie a lace or ribbon bow around the neck of the doll.

Step 9

Cuddle!

The Joys of Family Life

Beth and I are very lucky to live in a magnificent part of England; Devon has amazing countryside, gorgeous beaches and stunning moorland, so it's the perfect place for families to live and children to grow up. It is only fitting that living in such a wonderful and beautiful area, I want to introduce naturally beautiful fabrics to our family life.

I love making handmade clothes and bags for my children. My daughter (who is four going on fourteen!) just adores having a miniature version of everything I make and it's so easy to downsize all our projects and make matching sets.

Some of the projects we used in this chapter were chosen by my daughter. I asked her about all the things I have made her and which of these she likes the best. She is always very honest about what she does and doesn't like (sometimes a little too honest!) and quickly chose the aprons and the shopper. She really enjoys putting her apron on and helping me in the kitchen so it's a great way for us to spend quality time together.

Like me, she also has a passion for bags and I am always finding missing household items squirreled away in one of her bag collections! The shopper is well used and really does make shopping a stylish affair!

Beth and I feel that family life is what defines us, our projects, and our style. Modern living can be hectic, but surrounding ourselves with soothing fabrics and simple designs can help to bring a little calm and serenity back into all our lives.

Calmness and serenity.

Aprons

For Mother & Daughter

My daughters adore baking, so each Saturday morning we take time to cook something delicious for the weekend. Their favourite recipes are shortbread cookies and muffins (I like them too). We are a house full of very enthusiastic chefs and we're all a little bit messy in the kitchen, so aprons are essential apparel. I designed this matching pair to make our baking days even more special!

Master chefs in the making!

Step 1

Use the template supplied to cut the apron shape and pocket from the fabric.

Step 2

Fold over the top and bottom seams of the pocket and pin (don't worry about the sides as these will be hidden in the hem of the apron).

Step 3

Open the bias binding and align the edge of the binding with the top straight edge of the pocket, right sides together. Pin and sew along the binding crease. Tuck in the corners of the binding and repeat the process on the curved edges of the pocket. Sew the binding over the back of the fabric to complete the pocket.

Materials (Mother's Apron)

Template cut-out for Apron
75 x 55cm (29½ x 21¾in) of fabric for apron
25 x 55cm (9¼ x 21¾in) of fabric for pocket
85cm (33½in) of bias binding
150cm (59in) of ribbon for ties
2 decorative buttons

Materials (Child's Apron)

Template cut-out for Apron
50 x 35cm (19¾ x 13¾in) of fabric
120cm (47¼in) of ribbon for ties
180 x 10cm (70¾ x 4in) of fabric for ruched edging

Step 4

Place your pocket 15cm (6in) up from the bottom of your apron. Flip the pocket over so that the right sides are together, pin in place and sew the pocket base seam on the apron.

Step 5

Once the base of your pocket is attached, pin and sew the top of your pocket to your apron along the seam in the bias binding. Leave the curved edges unstitched.

Step 6

Find the middle line of your pocket and sew a vertical line from the top to the bottom to create two pocket sections.

Step 7

Cut 50cm (19¾in) of ribbon for your neck loop. Fold over a 1cm (½in) hem at the top of your apron. Place your ribbon 3cm (1¼in) in from each edge of the apron and fold over a 1cm (½in) hem again, enclosing your ribbon. Pin and sew the hem.

Step 8

Pin and sew a double hem (where you fold, then fold again so no raw edges are showing) on each of the side curved edges of your apron.

Step 9

Pin and sew a double hem down the remaining raw edges, folding in a 50cm (19¾in) piece of ribbon at each side (as done previously on the neck loop), about 1cm (½in) down from the curved edges.

Step 10

To finish, fold, pin and sew a double hem along the bottom of your apron.

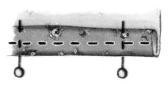

Too Cute!

For the children's apron we have used the basic apron template supplied, hemmed and attached the neck loop ribbon (about 40cm or 15¾in) as above in step 7, hemmed both scoops and added a cute ruffle around the rest of the apron, but don't forget to add your side ribbons (about 40cm (15¾in) each side). To see how to make the ruffle, see our easy but effective techniques section at the end of the book (page 92).

We have added buttons and a little padded dog to decorate our apron! This can be done at the end.

25

Stylish *Shopper*

I designed this lovely practical shopper because I wanted to have a really pretty bag to take with me to the local food market. In our house we are always running out of bread and milk so it is always with me, folded up in the bottom of my bag and ready for action. I also think it's important to try to remain as environmentally friendly as possible so using your shopper rather than plastic bags has got to be better for the planet. This design is easy to sew and can be made very quickly. Smaller versions can be made from scraps of fabric or you can go large to carry towels to the beach or books to the library.

Make shopping a stylish occasion!

Materials

2 pieces 10 x 100cm (4 x 39¼in) of fabric for handles

35 x 22cm (13¾ x 8¾in) of fabric for pocket

2 pieces 35 x 50cm (13¾ x 19¾in) of main fabric

2 pieces 35 x 50cm (13¾ x 19¾in) of lining fabric

1 button

65cm (25½in) of ribbon

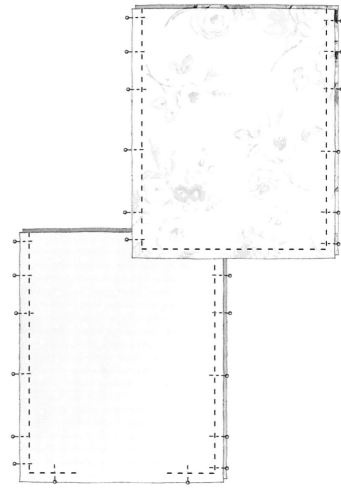

Step 1

Hem one long edge of the pocket fabric. Place the pocket fabric on the front of one of the main pieces, making sure that the sides and bottom are flush. Tack in place.

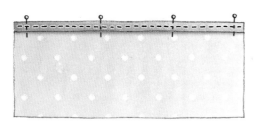

Step 2

Place the two main pieces of outer fabric right sides together. Pin and sew down both sides and along the bottom, securing the pocket in place. Repeat with the lining, leaving a 10cm (4in) gap in the centre at the bottom.

Step 3

Turn the main fabric the right way out and add your button to the top of the pocket.

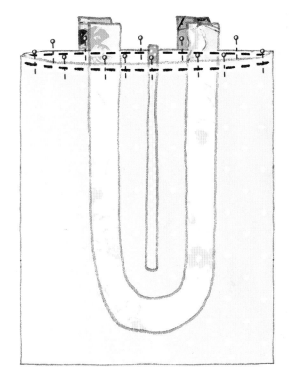

Step 4

To make the handles, fold in 3cm (1¼in) along one of the long edges and press. Fold the other long edge 1cm (½in) in and press. Fold this edge over again so it slightly overlaps the other side. Press, pin and sew three lines of stitching down the handles, one centrally and one either side.

Step 5

Slip the outer fabric inside the lining so the right sides are facing each other. Tuck the handles inside between the lining and the outer fabric as shown. Fold the ribbon in half and tuck the loop end in too. Pin and sew around the top rim of the bag.

Step 6

Reach through the gap in the lining and pull the bag through to turn it right sides out. Once you've done this you should iron the top seam flat before sewing around once more, about 2cm (¾in) from the top, to reinforce the handles. Sew up the hole in the lining.

Up-Cycle
Your Cardi

I had a wardrobe full of cardigans that were perfectly lovely (but that I'd grown a little tired of). I didn't want to give them away but I never seemed to wear them any more. Wardrobe space is at a premium in our house, so after a little bit of creative thinking I decided I would re-invent them. I collected some odd buttons to replace the rather dull-looking ones and decided that a corsage would give my rather plain cardis a fresh lease of life. Now I can't stop renovating and feel like I've got a whole new wardrobe of clothes for the price of a few buttons and a tiny piece of fabric!

Pimp your wardrobe!

Materials

1 plain cardigan, new or second-hand

About 6–10 buttons

2 squares of fabric 12 x 12cm (4¾ x 4¾in)

1 self-cover button and fabric to cover it

3 squares of complementary fabric 10 x 10cm
  (4 x 4in)

About 1m (1yd) of trimming

Step 1

Remove any old buttons from your cardigan and replace with the new buttons. We have used a selection of coloured fisheye buttons. It's great if you can find some vintage buttons in a market or from your granny's collection. (All grannies have a big tin of buttons!)

Step 2

Fold a 10cm (4in) square of fabric diagonally and then diagonally again. Sew a small running stitch from the right to the left-hand side of the bottom raw edge. Pull the thread tight and the fabric triangle should gather together, creating a petal/leaf shape. Knot the end of the thread so the petal keeps its shape. Repeat for the other two petals, or as many petals as you like. I think an odd number always looks better than an even number.

Step 3

Choose a self-cover button and an offcut of fabric to cover it in. Cut a roughly circular shape slightly larger than the button you are covering and ease the fabric over the button teeth, smoothing out any creases as you go. Next you can either use a self-cover button maker or a strong hand to push the button back into place, sealing the fabric.

Step 4

Sew the petals together and place the button in the middle. You can now add this to your cardigan.

Step 5

Measure the collar, cuffs or bottom of your cardigan and sew the trimming on to any of these areas.

Step 6

Create a pocket with the two 12cm (4¾in) squares, face right sides together and sew a 0.5cm (¼in) seam around the edges leaving a small 2cm (¾in) opening. Turn right side out through the gap and stitch a finishing stitch around all four edges of the pocket. Tack the pocket in place, and then sew around three edges, leaving the top edge open.

Step 7

Wear your cardi with pride!

SEW A LITTLE HAPPINESS

Top-Tip

You can add as many embellishments as you like using buttons, flower corsages, applique shapes and even embroidery thread.

The Easiest
Girl's Dress
in the World

I love this simple design and I love seeing my daughter wearing it, although she has taken to wearing it out in the garden with wellington boots! This straightforward project uses just one piece of fabric that you can cut to fit, so it suits almost any child size. I came up with the idea of making the dress using shirring elastic, which gathers up as you sew and creates a great 'smocking' effect, altering the shape of an otherwise square piece of fabric. If you are like me and just use your sewing machine on the same setting all the time, adjusting your machine can be quite fiddly and awkward to begin with so make sure you do a test before you start on the dress itself. Once you get the hang of this stitch, it's quite addictive!

A girl can never have too many dresses!

Step 1

Cut the bias binding in half, pin each piece along the long sides of the fabric and attach (see page 91).

Step 2

Thread your bobbin with the shirring elastic. It is best to do this by hand as it is important not to stretch the thread as it goes on to the bobbin.

Step 3

Set your sewing machine to a large zigzag stitch and a high tension. Using the sewing-machine foot as a guide, place it flush to the edge of the bias binding at one end of the fabric. Start your row with a backstitch to ensure that the elastic is anchored in place and sew a zigzag line the entire length of your fabric. Repeat the reverse stitch at the end of your row, securing the elastic.

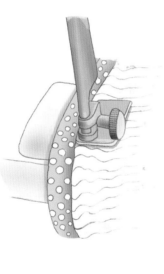

Step 4

Sew 15 rows in exactly the same way, always using your machine's foot as a guide, keeping it flush to the previous line. As you sew each row, ensure your fabric is kept taut. The shirring elastic will draw the fabric together.

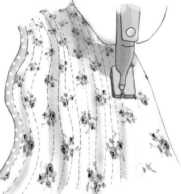

Materials

100 x 50cm (39¼ x 19¾in) of fabric
  (will fit up to age 7)
2m (79in) of bias binding
Shirring elastic
1m (1yd) of ribbon for ties
4 small buttons

Step 5

Using the hot, steam setting on your iron, press your dress on the stitched area and this will help the elastic to gather effectively.

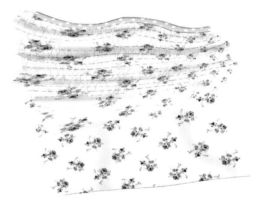

Step 6

Place the dress around your child and very carefully pin the two raw edges together to ensure you get a perfect fit. Cut off any excess. My daughter is nearly four years old and I cut off about 25cm (9¾in) from the edge.

Step 7

Place the wrong sides together and sew a French seam along the raw edge (see page 91).

Step 9

To finish, sew a button at the base of each of your four ties.

Step 8

Cut the ribbon into four equal pieces to create the shoulder ties, each 25cm (9¾in) long. Pin two in place at the front and two at the back, and then sew these securely. Tie each pair in a bow.

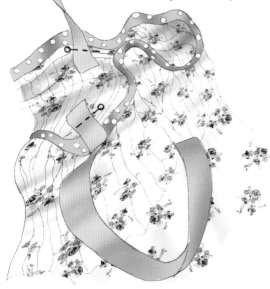

Step 10

Dress your daughter in it and take lots of cute photos!

Abbygale Homestyle

Home is where the heart is, that's what they say and I absolutely believe this to be true. I totally fell in love with my house the minute the estate agent showed me through the door. Within seconds of entering the living room, I was imagining my children playing happily in the garden, me at the stove cooking a hearty meal and romantic nights in front of the fire with my husband! Before long the beautiful little house on the hill was ours.

As soon as we moved in I set about filling it with cushions and quilts, made from scraps of vintage fabric I had been collecting for years. It was as if I had been saving them for this moment ... for my forever house! Emma added to my collection with a house-warming gift, a beautiful Union Jack handmade floor cushion (she always knows just what I like) and it wasn't long before our new house really felt like home.

Emma and I often like to give cushions as gifts (you can never have too many in our opinion)! Handmade items add such a personal touch and all of our home designs have been created with love and friendship in mind.

Taking Emma's Union Jack floor cushion as inspiration, we have created a dear little cushion for this chapter. It's one of our favourite projects in the book and is the epitome of British style. It takes pride of place on the sofa and looks fantastic with my husband's painting hanging on the wall behind.

We have been in our home for nearly a year now and our next project is the garden. My daughters have inherited their Mum and Dad's creative streak and have all types of ideas and plans for the outside space; dens and willow wigwams feature high on their wish list. We have already hung a swing seat from the eucalyptus tree and have decorated the winding little path to bluebell woods with metres of bunting.

Home is where the heart is!

Cosy Hot-Water Bottle Cover

My warm snuggly bed is my favourite place when outside it is cold and raining. But the worst thing about getting into bed on a winter's night is when the bed itself is cold. It always takes ages to warm up, a bit like taking a dip in the English Channel! Our hot-water bottle cover is so pretty, that it's now a permanent feature on our sofa and sits alongside the cushions.

Warm, snug and cosy!

Step 1

Use the templates to cut pieces A (front), B (top back) and C (bottom back) from the wadding, outer and lining fabrics.

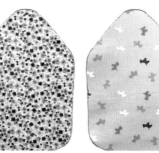

Materials

Template cut-outs for Hot-Water Bottle
50 x 60cm (19¾ x 23½in) of main fabric
50 x 60cm (19¾ x 23½in) of lining fabric
2 pieces 50 x 30cm (19¾ x 11¾in) of wadding
45cm (18in) of ribbon
1 button
Extra fabric scraps and button for corsage

Step 2

From the excess fabric, cut two circles of fabric, one 10cm (4in) and one 15cm (6in) in diameter. Around each circle, sew a running stitch 0.5cm (¼in) in from the edge. Once complete, pull both ends of the running-stitch thread, drawing the edges tightly into the centre to create the puff shape, then knot the thread.

Centre the smaller puff on the larger one and 20cm (8in) of folded ribbon on the back, then sew a button on top through all the layers.

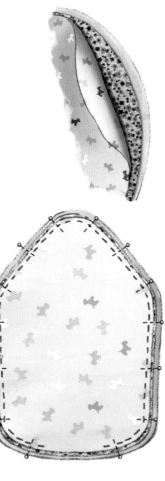

Step 3

Place both A (front) pieces of fabric right sides together and pin the wadding to the wrong side of the lining piece, ensuring you pin through all the layers.

Step 4

Sew a 1cm (½in) seam all the way around the shape, leaving a 10cm (4in) opening at the bottom. Trim the excess fabric and wadding. Turn your fabric right sides out by pulling through the gap in the seam. Sew your corsage to the front of piece A.

Step 5

Repeat steps three and four with pieces B and C.

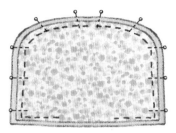

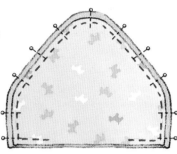

Step 6

It is really important to press each piece as you work to achieve a crisp finish.

Step 7

Cut 15cm (6in) of ribbon, loop it over and tuck the cut ends into the open seam of piece B. Pin it in place. Using your ribbon as a guide, work out the positioning of your button and sew it in place.

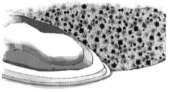

Step 8

Using the longest stitch length, close any open gaps on pieces B and C. Tuck any open fabric into the seam and sew across the width of the pieces starting and finishing 1cm (½in) in from each end.

Step 9

Pin piece C on to piece A and sew a 1cm (½in) seam around the edge, ensuring you close the gap at the bottom of piece A. Reinforce your stitching at each end.

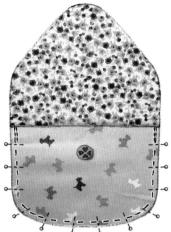

Step 10

Pin piece B to piece A. This will overlap piece C. Loop a 10cm (4in) piece of ribbon and pin it between pieces A and B at the top of your hot-water bottle cover. Finish by sewing a 1cm (½in) seam around the edge, starting and stopping where the seam on piece C begins and ends. This should leave you with a small flap.

The front of your hot-water bottle cover should have a continuous stitch all the way around.

Union Jack
Cushion

Cushions are a great way to change the whole feel of a room at very little cost. With just a few pieces of fabric you can transform a tired-looking sofa, cheer up a chair, or beautify your bed. What's more, they're easy to make and would be an ideal place to start if you're new to sewing. This Union Jack cushion would be a great addition to any room and can easily be coordinated with your existing colour scheme.

Cheer up a chair!

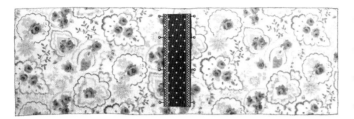

Step 1

Fold the large panel of fabric, halving the longest length. Find the centre line and press so you can use it as a guide.

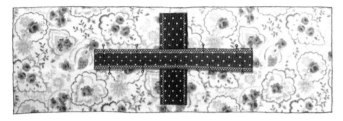

Step 2

Place the 8 x 28cm (3¼ x 11in) red strip centrally over the centre line of the panel and pin it in place. Use a medium-sized zigzag stitch to attach it. Pin the second red strip in a central, horizontal position to create a cross shape. Use the zigzag stitch to attach it.

Step 3

Take your four rectangles and cut into eight right-angled triangles. Use the iron-on webbing to attach each triangle to the cushion panel in the formation shown in the illustration. Cut your ribbon to the right sizes once the triangles are in place. Use zigzag stitch to attach them.

Materials

108 x 34cm (42½ x 13½in) of fabric

30cm (12in) zip

1 strip of red fabric 8 x 40cm (3¼ x 15¾in)

1 strip of red fabric 8 x 28cm (3¼ x 11in)

4 rectangles in complementary fabrics 8 x 16cm (3¼ x 6¼in) (preferably not red)

About 1m (1yd) of red ribbon

About 50 x 30cm (19¾ x 11¾in) of iron-on webbing

30 x 50cm (11¾ x 19¾in) cushion pad

Step 4

With the long piece of fabric laid out flat and positioned with the right side facing you, fold each side in equally so the raw edges meet in the middle. This will be where you will attach the zip. Pin and sew the right side of one zip edge to the right side of your fabric raw edge. When you get near to the pull, unzip slightly to allow your sewing machine enough space to continue. You may wish to use a zipper foot if you have one, or simply move your needle to the furthest left position.

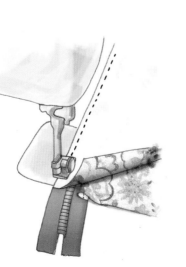

Top-Tip
Use pinking shears to add a decorative edge to all your pieces.

Step 5

Pin and sew the opposite right-side raw edge to the right side of the zip. Remember to move the pull to allow your sewing machine access all the way along this seam. Each end of the zip will be sewn into the seam, top and bottom.

Step 6

Make sure your cushion is inside out with the zip in the centre. Pin the raw edges of the bottom of the cushion cover together and sew a 1.5cm (¾in) seam. Stitch back and forth over the bottom of your zip a few times and cut off the excess.

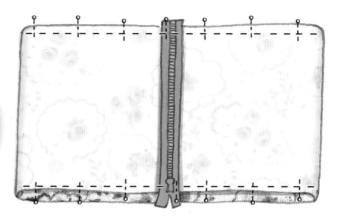

Step 7

Before you sew the top seam, undo your zip to the halfway position. Now pin the top edge and sew a 1.5cm (¾in) seam across.

Step 8

The inside of your cushion cover will have a lot of thread ends. Snip these off to ensure they don't catch in the zip. Turn out the right way through the open zip.

Step 9

Insert a cushion pad and put your cushion on your sofa. You will be the envy of all your friends!

Delightful Doorstop

I love filling my home with handmade treasures. It's always these little touches that people notice when they come round. I find people really appreciate being given such beautiful objects as gifts. This is the perfect project to use up scraps of your favourite fabrics, and even if you don't ever use it for the purpose it was intended it still adds style to your home.

A charming addition to any house!

Step 1

Decorate the front square panel of your doorstop with buttons or any embellishments you like.

Step 2

Sew the two squares and two rectangles together, with right sides facing, along the 20cm (8in) edge to create one long piece of fabric (see Illustration). Use a 1cm (½in) seam allowance.

Step 3

Snip the corners off each seam top and bottom. Iron the seams flat. This will help when placing the panels neatly on the top and bottom of your doorstop.

Step 4

Now sew the outside edges of the long panel together, right sides facing, to create a box shape. Remember to tidy up these seams by snipping the corners.

Materials

2 squares of cotton fabric 20 x 20cm (8 x 8in)

4 rectangles of cotton fabric 10 x 20cm (4 x 8in)

30cm (11¾in) length of webbing

2kg (4½lb) of dried beans for filling

Embroidery thread for decorative stitching

Buttons or other embellishments (optional)

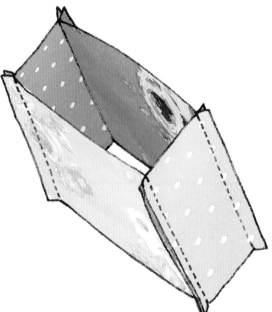

Step 5

Take another rectangle of fabric for the base and pin one side centrally to one of the side panels with right sides together. Where the fabric overlaps at the corners (due to the seam allowance), pinch a small triangle to allow for extra fabric on the corner and pin in place. Continue to pin the base to every side of the doorstop, pinching at every corner.

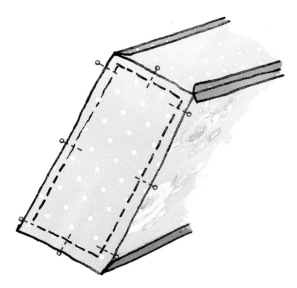

Step 6

Once the base of your door stop is completely pinned to the front, back and sides, sew together creating an open box shape. As you approach the pinched corners, sew up to 1cm (½in) before the end of the fabric, keep the needle down, release the presser foot and turn the fabric. Put the presser foot back down and continue sewing.

Step 7

Pin the webbing to the right side of each of the rectangular side panels. Now pin the final rectangular panel over the webbing to make the top of the doorstop, in the same way as you pinned on the base panel but leaving a 10cm (4in) gap along the long side to allow for filling.

Step 8

Turn your doorstop right side out by pulling it through the gap you have left. Poke out the corners. Your doorstop is now ready for filling. Pour the beans in through the hole until it is three-quarters full.

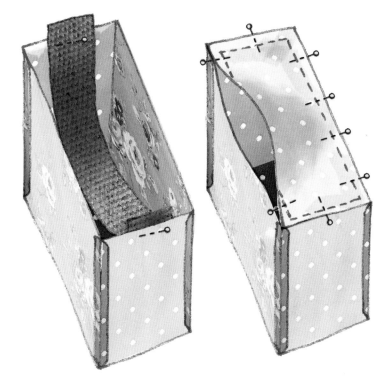

Step 9

Using an embroidery thread, sew blanket stitch around the front square, closing up the opening at the top (see page 91). Repeat on the back if you wish.

Festive Stocking

December is my favourite time of year. I love winter walks with friends and family, cosy evenings sitting around the fire with my loved ones and, of course, decorating our home with festive treats. Last Christmas was so special as it was the first one in our new house. It was a real joy to design a Christmas stocking to hang above our fireplace and it added such a homely touch to our living room.

Spreading joy, love and laughter!

Step 1

Fold both pieces of fabric in half so that they measure 35cm (13¾in) wide by 50cm (19¾in) high. Place your template cut-outs on top of the two pieces of folded fabric and pin them firmly in place. Carefully cut around your stocking shapes to create both outer and lining pieces.

Step 2

Remove the paper templates and pin all the stocking parts to each other (right sides together). Ensure that you have chosen the coordinating fabric for the heel, toe and cuff.

Step 3

Sew the stocking shapes together, taking a 1cm (½in) seam allowance. Sew the cuff, toe and heel to the main body of the stocking and repeat the process on the lining fabric. You will end up with four stocking shapes.

Step 4

Now place the two outer fabric stocking parts right sides together. Pin and sew around the stocking, leaving the top of it open. Repeat with the lining fabric. Remember to do a couple of reverse stiches at the beginning and end to prevent the seam from coming undone.

Materials

Template cut-outs for Festive Stocking
35 x 100cm (13¾ x 39¼in) of main fabric
35 x 100cm (13¾ x 39¼in) of lining fabric
24cm (9½in) of ribbon

Step 5

Turn the outer stocking the right way round. Iron both pieces then carefully fit the lining inside the outer stocking.

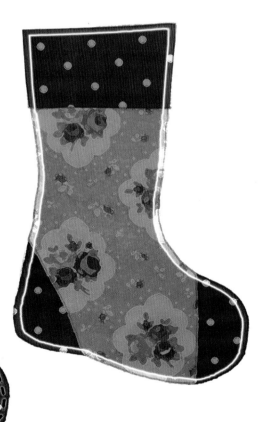

Step 6

Tuck in both raw edges around the top rim of your stocking by about 2cm (¾in).

Step 7

Fold the ribbon in half and push the cut ends in between the two folded edges. Pin in place. Top stitch or blanket stitch around the stocking rim to seal the edges (see page 91 for details).

Step 8

Hang up and wait for Santa!

Top-Tip

Why not attach a bell on to your stocking, so you will hear Santa coming!

No-sew gift idea!

Wrap your gifts in fabric and ribbon, then attach a little label with a suggestion of what you can make with the fabric you have used as the wrapping.

A Woman's Work is Never Done

Beth and I are fortunate enough to have our own gorgeous little studio in Cockington; a picturesque village in the English countryside with old thatched cottages and charming scenery. Working in a place like this is like taking a step back in time. Unfortunately, in order to do any type of business we are all reliant, to some degree, on the trappings of the twenty-first century world.

The projects we have chosen for this chapter are all ideas that make working life easier or more attractive. The mobile-phone and tablet cases will both help increase the enjoyment of using these gadgets; softening the boundary between the modern and the traditional. Creating a gorgeous cover or case is a great way to protect and personalise any mobile device. And, the handbag is the perfect accessory; big enough to fit in all the essentials, yet still elegant, portable and chic.

We have a small collection of vintage sewing machines and whilst these are really beautiful as pieces of design, we rarely actually use them for sewing projects. Most modern day machines are reliable at the expense of being attractive and can often look clumsy and gauche when placed in the context of your carefully chosen interiors. The cover we have designed in this chapter allows you keep your sewing machine ready for action and retain pride of place without standing out like a sore thumb.

We are both very passionate about our work. After all, it's pretty difficult not to feel inspired when you're creating original things from beautiful fabrics. Once you've made a few of the projects in this book we think you'll agree that it is far more pleasurable to have something handmade and organic in your life, than something mass produced and generic.

Beautiful fabric is our remedy for
the harsh digital age!

Country-Style *Handbag*

I adore this traditional handbag, it's just the right size to hold all my essentials, as well as all those extras that my children seem to ask me to look after! Needless to say, I use it often and it seems to suit all occasions. I recently made an evening version of this bag using a blue velvet for the outer and a patterned silk for the inner. I finished it with some beading and a glass button to add a touch of extra sparkle.

Perfect for town or country, day or night!

Step 1

Use the template provided to cut four pieces of fabric, two for the outside and two for the lining. Cut four strips, each 8cm (3¼in) wide and about 60cm (23¾in) long, from the remainder of the fabric for the handle straps (two from the outer fabric and two from the lining as shown). Pin the two main lining pieces right sides together, then sew up the left and right edges. Repeat with the outer pieces.

Materials

Template cut-outs for Handbag
2 pieces 70 x 60 cm (27½ x 23½in) of outer fabric
2 pieces 70 x 60 cm (27½ x 23½in) of lining fabric
1 button
20cm (7¾in) of ribbon
Safety pin

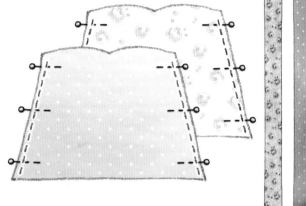

Step 2

Turn the outer fabric right side out and sew a button centrally on the front about 10cm (4in) from the top. Then turn the outer fabric inside out again to match the lining. Sew along the bottom of each piece, leaving a gap in the lining for turning right side out later.

Step 3

To create the bag's depth, take the outer part and pull out the bottom two corners, then sew across each one 4cm (1½in) from the corner point. Once sewn, trim off the triangles as shown and repeat this process with the lining.

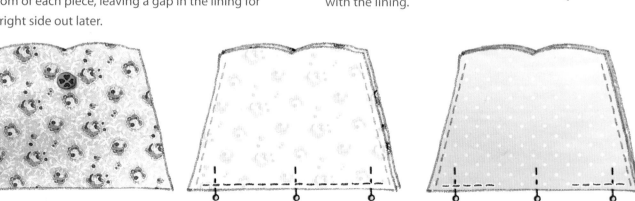

Step 4

Make a handle by placing a strip of lining fabric and a strip of outer fabric right sides together, then pin and sew as shown. Pull the handle through itself so that it's the right way out (attaching a safety pin to the end will make it a lot easier to pull through). Repeat this process with the other handle, then iron them flat and top stitch down each of the edges for strength.

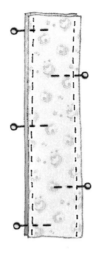

Step 6

Once all the edges are neat and flat, iron around the top edges and top stitch around the top rim of the bag. Try to stay as close to the edge as possible without straying off the fabric – take your time and the result will look really professional! Sew up the hole in the lining to finish.

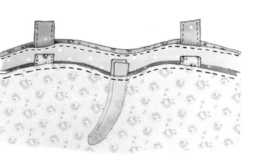

Step 5

Tuck the lining inside the outer bag, making sure the right sides of the fabric are facing each other. Fold the ribbon in half and tuck the loop end between the lining and the outer bag on the opposite side to the button. Tuck the handles inside, making sure they are positioned centrally (as shown above). Ensure that the corresponding fabrics of the handle and bag are facing each other, then pin and sew around the top rim of the bag. Once you have checked that all the seams are closed, remove the pins and carefully turn the bag right side out by pulling the handles through the hole you left in the lining.

A girl can never have too many bags!

Vintage Floral
Phonecase

Our vintage-style floral phonecases were one of our very first designs. These beautiful little fabric cases fit most phone types and are very simple to make. Mobile phones are now an integral part of family life; whether for taking photos, sending emails, entertaining the children or even making calls. We think our cases add an organic touch and a dash of vintage flair to 21st century living!

Making the modern world pretty!

Step 1

Use the template pattern provided and cut two pieces of fabric, one from the main fabric and one from the lining.

Step 2

Lay out the outer fabric and sew on the button and one part of the Velcro dot as shown below. Position the Velcro so that when the flap is closed it lies directly underneath the button.

Step 3

Lay out the lining fabric and sew on the other part of the Velcro in the same position as the button.

Materials

Template cut-outs for Phonecase
12 x 37cm (4¾ x 14½in) of outer fabric
12 x 37cm (4¾ x 14½in) of lining fabric
1 button
8cm (3¼in) of ribbon
1 hook-and-loop (Velcro) dot

Step 4

Place the inner and outer fabrics right sides together. Fold the piece of ribbon in half and tuck the loop end between the two fabrics at the top of the flap, leaving about 1cm (½in) poking out at the top. Secure this with a pin, making sure it is central, then pin down the sides as shown.

Step 5

Sew around three sides as shown, about 7mm (¼in) in from the edge. Be sure to leave the base open for turning through when you've finished. Once you've done this, remove the pins and turn the case through to reveal the right side. You may find it helpful to use something to poke out the corners. We used the end of a chopstick but anything thin and blunt should do the trick.

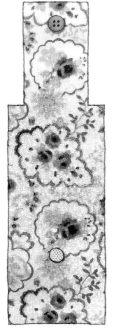

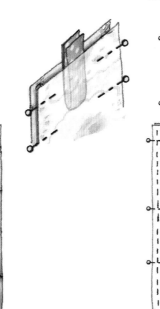

Step 6

Fold the open end in on itself by 1.5cm (¾in) before ironing it down nice and flat, ready for sewing. Do not iron the Velcro patch as it will melt! Carefully iron the rest of the case to get all the edges flat.

Step 7

Sew around all the sides about 3mm (⅛in) from the edges. Turn the bottom up to meet the base of the flap and sew down each side, following the existing stitch line. It's worth sewing this twice and also reinforcing at each end.

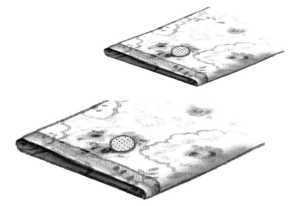

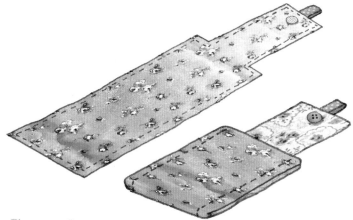

Step 8

Turn the phonecase the right way out and give it a final run over with the iron.

Notebook cover

Keep your life in order with a fabric-covered notebook that matches your bag. Cut your fabric slightly larger than the book's cover and use a fabric glue to keep it in place, neatly folding the edges over the inside of the front and back covers.

Trendy Fabric
Tablet Case

My house seems to be filled with gadgets! I use them daily and have come to rely on my tablet more and more. My busy schedule somehow seems less daunting when it's all organised in one place with little chimes and alarms alerting me to the next task of the day. I wanted to give it a personal touch and also keep sticky fingers away from the screen, so I set about making this cute case. It's so quick to sew and makes the perfect partner to the phonecase.

A cosy cover for my technology!

How much fabric do I need?

Add 5cm (2in) to the width and triple the length of your tablet. Our tablet measures 25cm (9¾in) long and 19cm (7½in) wide, so we have cut our fabric to 75 x 24cm (29½ x 9½in).

Step 1

Cut the interfacing, outer and inner fabrics to the calculated size. Iron the interfacing to the wrong side of the lining fabric. The interfacing makes your case a bit sturdier. Try using quilter's wadding instead if you have no interfacing.

Materials

About 80cm x 25cm (31½ x 9¾in) of outer fabric
About 80cm x 25cm (31½ x 9¾in) of lining fabric
Embellishments (buttons etc.)
About 10cm (4in) of ribbon
Hook-and-loop (Velcro) dots
Medium-strength interfacing

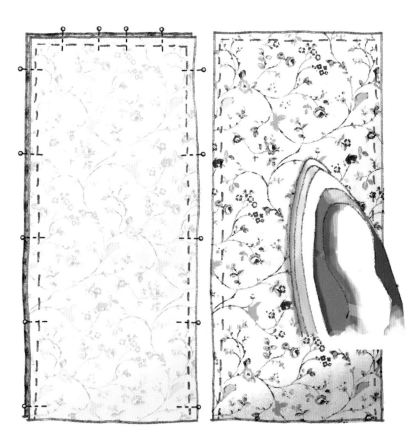

Step 2

Sew any embellishments on to what will be the outer flap of your case. You may want to place your tablet centrally and fold the bottom (pocket) section up and the top (flap) section down for more accurate positioning.

Step 3

Pin the outer fabric and lining fabric (with interfacing attached) right sides together then sew a 1cm (½in) seam around three sides, leaving the top flap section open. Snip the two bottom corners of the seam allowances off to allow for smoother corners when turning the right way out.

Step 4

Turn the fabric the right way out, making sure you poke the corners out and iron again to achieve a crisp finish.

Step 5

Place your tablet centrally on the fabric and pull up the closed bottom section so it totally covers your device. Pin it in place.

Step 6

Fold the open-seamed flap over and tuck in the raw edges. At this point you can adjust the length of the flap to suit your taste. If you find you have too much fabric you can cut your flap to the length that you require. Once you have the preferred size, tuck in the raw edges, pin together and unfold.

Step 7

Sew the hook part of two Velcro dots on to the lining of the flap, one on each side, about 4cm (1½in) from the edge of the flap. Avoid stitching through the front of your flap. Sew the loop Velcro dots on the outside of the pocket section of the case so that they meet. Fold your ribbon in half and tuck in 2cm (¾in) of the folded ribbon into the open edge of flap. Pin in place.

Step 8

Sew a 1cm (½in) seam around three sides of your case, sealing the pocket and pinned seam in place. If you find that the fabric is too wide and your tablet is not snug, adjust your seam allowance.

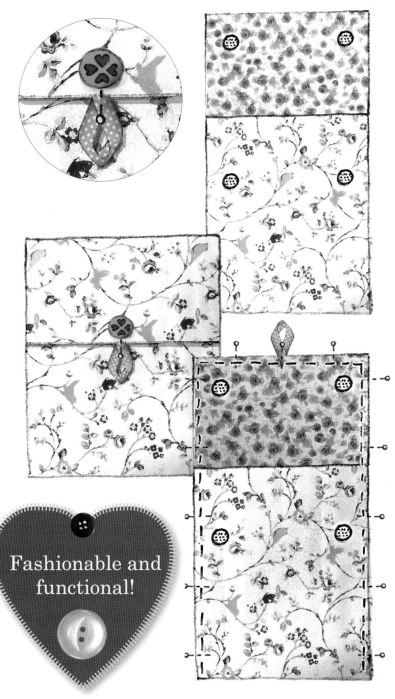

Fashionable and functional!

Sewing Machine Cover

I have five sewing machines: three of them are beautiful vintage models that look stunning – two old Singers and a wonderful ornate Jones. They are temperamental, heavy and not at all practical, but I love looking at them! I love the feel of sewing with the treadle and the soft sound when stitching. However, my two most used and practical machines are not blessed in the style department! They are bulky, faceless and plastic but I use them all the time because they are so reliable, which is why I included the sewing-machine cover as a project. It is perfect – easy to put on and take off and pretty to look at. This is a wonderful way to hide your machine when not in use and really fun to put together.

I wish I could sew all day!

Emma Curtis
Thread Lane
Sewing Heaven

Step 1

Work out the cover size required by measuring your sewing machine's width and adding a further 10cm (4in). Next measure from the back base, over the top to the front base of your machine; the fabric should just touch the surface on which your sewing machine sits on each side. Cut two pieces of fabric based on this rectangular shape – one for the outer cover and one for the lining.

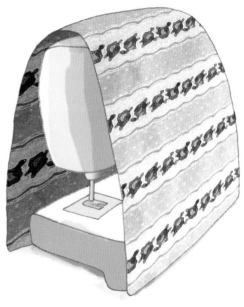

Step 2

We created a letter design on the outside of our cover using inkjet fabric, although any appliqué picture can be applied. Use a felt rectangle as a canvas for the appliqué panel. Let your creative side go wild: use embellishments, vary your stitch pattern, use photographs and any left-over scraps of fabric. You could even let the children have a go with some fabric glue to create an appliqué scene!

Materials

About 60 x 80cm (23½ x 31½in) of outer fabric
About 60 x 80cm (23½ x 31½in) of lining fabric
Inkjet fabric
24 x 32cm (9½ x 12½in) of felt
Wadding
Embroidery thread
120cm (47¼in) of pom-pom trimming
2m (2¼yd) of ribbon
Embellishments of your choice

Step 3

Once you are happy with the design, place some wadding behind the felt panel and pin it to the front of the cover along with any other embellishments you'd like to add; use a zigzag stitch to attach the panel. To decorate, we cut out a rose from some leftover fabric and made a flower puff (see page 92). Use embroidery thread to hand sew your remaining embellishments in place.

Step 4

Face the right sides of the outer and the lining pieces together and place the pom-pom trimming, sandwiched between the two layers, at each of the shorter ends. Pin in place, making sure the edge of the trimming is flush to the edge of the fabric and that the pom-poms are facing inwards. This will ensure that they hang down when you turn your cover right side out.

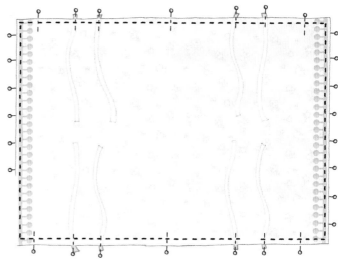

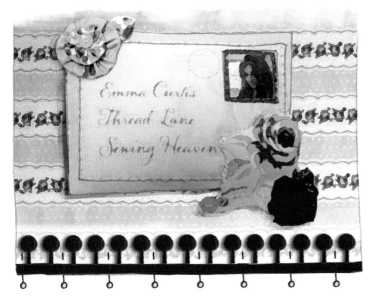

Step 5

Cut the ribbon into eight equal lengths of 25cm (9¾in). Fold your cover in half and decide where you would like the ribbon ties to go (see the illustration top right for guidance). Place each piece of ribbon between the outer and the lining fabric and pin in place. You should have four pieces on each side.

Step 6

Sew around all four sides, securing the ribbon ties and pom-pom trimming in place. Leave a 15cm (6in) gap for turning through.

Step 7

Turn the cover the right way out through the gap, and then fold the raw edges in. Press and sew a finishing stitch all the way around your cover just inside the edge.

Top Tip

You could use your appliqué panels for all sorts of items: canvas artwork, cushions, tablemats and even children's clothes.

An English Country Garden Party

Long summer evenings in Devon are hard to beat and enjoying quality time with family and friends is a tonic for the soul! Our garden is the perfect setting for a summer garden party. Of course, the British weather is not always conducive to holding such events but we are never deterred by a shower or two!

Despite having a limited knowledge of plants I have longed for a large garden for many years. Luckily my Mum and Dad are expert gardeners and are always on hand to give us their green-fingered advice. Dad has fantastic landscaping ideas and Mum is able to grow anything from cuttings and seeds. My latest plan is to create a lavender path which meanders gently through the garden, fringed with yards of pretty handmade bunting.

In this chapter, Emma and I have had great fun designing projects for indoors and out. Our fabulous and functional table runner and matching place mats are amongst my favourite projects in the book. They are just so easy to make and look simply divine when laid out for an afternoon picnic in the garden. For extra comfort, you could also try making our traditional English patchwork bean bag. These are so popular with my children and their friends I hardly ever have the opportunity to sit on one myself!

Our teacosy design is classically British and bound to attract some admiring comments from your tea-party guests. Once you've made a cosy for your pot, why not try our Devon cream tea recipe for that quintessentially English experience!

Devon Cream Tea Recipe

Preheat oven to gas mark 7 / 220 degrees C. Put **400g (14oz) self-raising flour, 1 tsp of baking powder** and a **pinch of salt** into a mixing bowl. Rub **50g (1¾oz) of butter** into the mix, until it looks like breadcrumbs. Add **3 tbsp of caster sugar** and mix. Gradually add **250ml (8¾fl oz) of milk** and fold with a wooden spoon until your mixture forms a dough. Turn out and use a cookie cutter to cut the scones. Brush with leftover milk and place on a greased baking tray. Bake for 10–12mins. Eat warm with lashings of **Devon clotted cream and strawberry jam.**

Picnic Table
Runner & Mats

A beautifully set table makes a real impact when entertaining and adds to the ambience of any event. I can then serve up my favourite simple dishes and my guests are still impressed! The beauty of the table runner and place mat set is that it's made from panels so you don't need huge pieces of fabric. I also like to make everyone's place mat slightly different and even personalise them for special occasions. Freshly cut flowers and mismatched crockery give a vintage twist to any dinner party!

A cosy home is one where nothing matches!

Step 1

Join three strips of coordinating fabric right sides together along the longest sides, taking a 1cm (½in) seam allowance. Repeat this process to create three blocks of three strips.

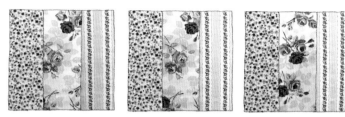

Step 2

Press your blocks, ironing the seams flat, and sew them together, turning the centre block so the strips are going in a different direction to the blocks on either side.

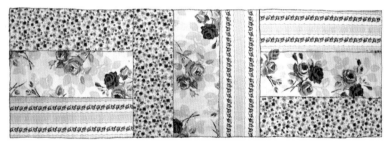

Step 3

Cut the ribbon in half. Pin and sew the two pieces of ribbon along the two seams either side of your central panel.

Step 4

Sew a hem around all four sides of the table runner.

Materials for Table Runner:

9 strips of fabric 18 x 50cm (7 x 19¾in)
1m (1yd) of ribbon

Step 1

Take two fabric strips, place them right sides together, then pin and sew one long side seam. Press the seam flat.

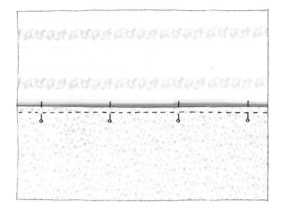

Materials for Four Table Mats:

8 strips of fabric 18 x 50cm (7 x 19¾in)
4 lengths of ribbon 65cm (25½in) long

Step 2

Starting at the left-hand side of your mat, pin the ribbon along the central seam, ensuring you allow an extra 1cm (½in) on the left side to tuck into your hem. When you have pinned to about 40cm (15¾in) across, make three finger-sized loops of ribbon and pin them in place, then continue pinning the ribbon along the central seam.

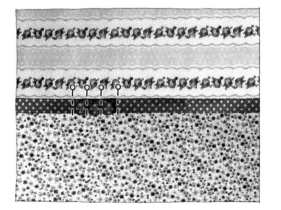

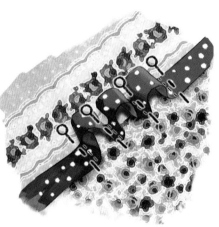

Step 3

Stitch two lines along the ribbon until you reach the loops. Stitch a vertical line at the start of the first loop, then a vertical line in between each loop and another at the end of the third loop. Continue sewing two lines to the right-hand edge. Tuck the remaining ribbon around the edge.

Step 4

Hem all of the raw edges, neatly enclosing the ribbon at each end.
Repeat all of the above steps for the other three mats. Mix and match your fabrics, or introduce a new fabric for the other mats.

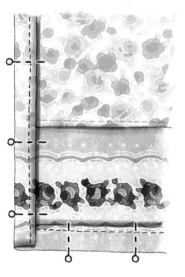

Tip-Top Teacosy

Tea with friends is always a delight, especially when there's an opportunity to enjoy a few sweet treats and a good gossip! Each month my girlfriends and I take it in turns to bake cakes and have a get together. My latest bake was a traditional Devon Cream Tea (recipe on page 75). I wanted everything to look perfect, so I designed this cute teacosy as the centrepiece of my table. It's really simple to make, looks great and keeps your tea piping hot!

Makes every tea-time a bit special!

Step 1

Use the template supplied to cut your teacosy shape out of the fabric and wadding – two pieces of lining, two pieces of outer fabric and two pieces of wadding.

Step 2

To create your decorative teabags cut an 8cm (3¼in) diameter circle in two contrasting fabrics and an 8cm (3¼in) square in the same two fabrics (we have used a tea cup and saucer fabric).

Step 3

For each teabag, face right sides together and sew a 0.5cm (¼in) seam around the edges, leaving a small 2cm (¾in) opening at the centre top to allow you to turn your teabags right side out.

Turn out and fill with the excess wadding. Cut the 40cm (15¾in) of ribbon in half, tuck the cut ends into each of the 2cm (¾in) gaps left in your teabags and pin. Sew a finishing stitch around all the edges of each teabag, ensuring that the gap is closed neatly.

Step 4

Create your pocket in the same way, by sewing the right sides together and leaving a small gap of 2cm (¾in). Turn right side out through the gap and work a finishing stitch around all four edges of the pocket.

Materials

Template cut-outs for Teacosy

100 x 30cm (39½ x 11¾in) of outer fabric

100 x 30cm (39½ x 11¾in) of lining fabric

100 x 30cm (39½ x 11¾in) of wadding

80cm (31½in) of 18mm (¾in) bias binding

80cm (31½in)of ric-rac for decoration

40cm (15¾in) of ribbon for teabag strings

2 fabric squares 11 x 11cm (4¼ x 4¼in) for the pocket

2 fabric offcuts at least 8 x 8cm (3¼ x 3¼in) for
  each teabag

Step 5

Cut the ric-rac in half and place one piece on the front of the outer fabric along with your pocket. Pin in place. Pin the remaining ric-rac in the same position on the back piece of the outer fabric. Sew the ric-rac and pocket in place, leaving the top of your pocket open.

Pin your hanging teabag ribbons to the centre top of your teacosy.

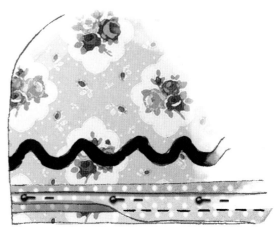

Step 7

Pin the front and back outer pieces of your teacosy right sides together and sew a 1cm (½in) seam around the arc, remembering to sew the hanging teabags in place. Turn the right way out.

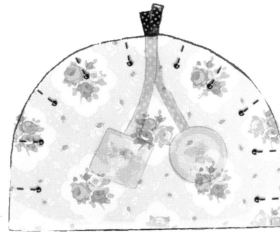

Step 9

Tuck the lining inside the outer part of the teacosy. Pin the bias binding in place around the outside bottom edge, leaving a 5mm (¼in) gap at the bottom. Unfold the binding and sew along the crease mark. Cut off any excess from the bottom of your cosy to remove the bulk.

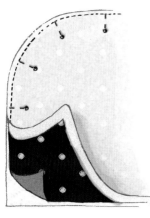

Step 8

Place the lining pieces right sides together, sandwich them between the two pieces of wadding and pin. Sew a 1cm (½in) seam through all four layers, around the arc of the teacosy.

Step 10

Fold the unstitched edge of the binding around the bottom of your cosy and pin to the inside lining. Finish stitching the binding in place by hand or on a sewing machine (see page 91).

Traditional
English Patchwork Bean Bag

I recently joined a quilting group for which a few of the mums from the children's school get together one evening a week to make quilts. It's a perfect way to use up pieces of fabric that you have lying around (and I have cupboards full of fabric). One of the first projects we made was a pincushion based on traditional English patchwork. I loved the technique so much that I decided to make a giant version, using it as a bean bag for the house and garden. Sewing it together is quick and easy, but the hexagons need to be carefully measured and cut in order to make them easy to piece together. It's worth it though, as the results are amazing!

Patchwork is addictive!

Step 1

Print out or photocopy
20 paper hexagon
templates and 6 square
templates on any paper
– the thinner the better.

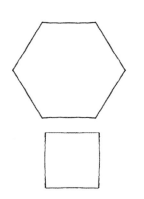

Step 2

Place each template on
a piece of fabric and cut
around the templates,
leaving a margin of
about 2cm (¾in) of fabric
all round.

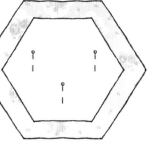

Step 3

Fold the extra fabric over
the edge of the paper
template and tack in
place. Don't worry about
being neat; all these
stitches and the paper will
be removed eventually.
Press with a hot iron to
make sure all the edges
are crisp. Repeat this for
all 20 hexagons and
6 squares.

Materials

Template cut-outs for Bean Bag pieces
Thin paper for templates
A selection of fabrics (we have used 6 different fabrics) :
    about 30 x 140cm (11¾ x 55in) of each
An old net curtain (optional)
About 1m (1yd) cubed of bean-bag filling

Step 4

You will need
to create two
sections, the
first made up
13 hexagons
and 6 squares
(see A) and the
second with
the remaining 7
hexagons (see B).

A

B

It is a good idea to lay
the fabric shapes out
on the floor to avoid
too many pattern
repeats before you
start sewing.

Step 5

When you are ready to start sewing, place the shapes you are joining right sides together and allow a 1cm (½in) seam. Sew along one edge of each shape and gradually build up the sections. When sewing into the corners, try to do this neatly to avoid bulk by keeping your needle down, lifting your presser-foot up and turning before placing the foot down and continuing to sew. Use a small stitch as this will make your bean bag more durable.

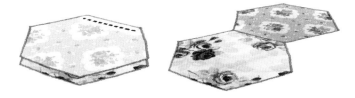

Step 6

Once you have joined the two sections, remove the tacking stitches and paper. This is a bit fiddly, but the paper and stitches should just rip out.

Step 7

Now it is time to join your two sections together. As before, place the right sides together along the ironed hems and sew using a 1cm (½in) seam. Leave two hexagon edges open.

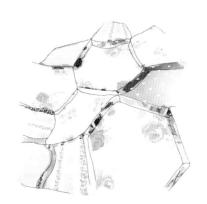

Step 8

Turn the bean bag the right way out and fill with the bean-bag filling. If you like, you can create a lining to place inside your bean-bag outer, to avoid any bean spillages. Make this with an old net curtain before adding the filling.

Step 9

Carefully sew up the open sides.

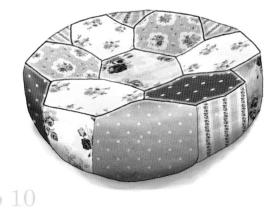

Step 10

Sit down and relax on your fantastic new bean bag!

Beautiful Bunting

Bunting is a permanent feature in our house, as it's such a cheerful thing to have hanging around the place. I refuse to have it sitting in a box and only brought out for parties – so I have it up all year round and it always makes me smile. It looks great hung between trees in the garden and is a pretty addition to a child's bedroom. As with all of our projects, bunting is a lovely gift idea, especially when it is personalised. I've added my daughters' names in felt lettering on theirs and they love them!

Why just save it for parties?

Materials

Fabric scraps – a rectangle of fabric 50 x 30cm (19¾ x 11¾in) will be enough for 2 flags)

Small buttons

Ribbon – you can make your bunting any length: allow 25cm (10in) of ribbon for every flag

Step 1

Create your flag template by drawing a simple triangle. The central line of the triangle from top to bottom should measure 29cm (11½in) and the width of the base 18cm (7in). Cut out four triangles from each piece of fabric.

Step 2

Choose the fabrics you would like to place together for each flag. This could be random or kept in an organised pattern. Place the triangular fabric pairs right sides together. Pin and sew around the two long sides, keeping the top side open.

Step 3

Turn the fabric triangles the right way out and press. You may need to push the point out with a knitting needle or something similar. Carefully tuck in both raw edges on the top edge and top stitch around the whole triangle to close the opening and create a neat finish.

Step 4

Pin your triangles on to the ribbon at regular intervals. We recommend every 15cm (6in), leaving 30cm (12in) at either end. Sew in place once you are happy with the spacing.

Step 5

Decorate your bunting further by adding buttons – two on each triangle.

Easy Embellishment Techniques

Bias binding

Bias binding is great for hiding a raw edge and adding an extra-special touch to a boring hem. There are lots of beautiful patterned bindings available and you can even make your own.

Open out the binding and place it flush to the edge of the fabric, right sides together. Use the crease of the binding as a marker, then sew along this line. Fold over the binding to the other side of the fabric, removing any excess bulk as necessary. You can then sew this in place by hand (being careful to avoid any stitches showing through by using a slipstitch). Alternatively, use the machine to catch the back of the binding by using the point where binding and fabric meet on the right side as a guide. You need to have slightly more binding on the inside than the outside for this method, but I much prefer using the machine to hand sewing.

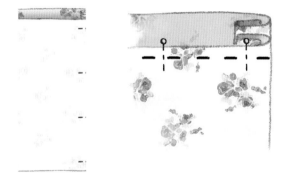

French seam

A French seam doubles the seam strength so is ideal for use on clothing. It also prevents fraying and looks neat and professional. This technique is perfect for unlined items so you avoid seeing all those tatty raw edges.

You start a French seam by sewing the wrong sides together. Now trim the seam allowance to remove excess bulk. Fold the fabric over so you have the right sides together and sew again.

Blanket stitch

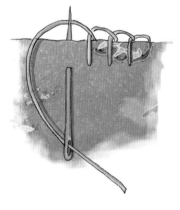

Once you learn how to blanket stitch you will want to use it to edge everything. It is simple, fun and you can do it while watching the television or in your lunch hour. All you need is a large-eyed needle and embroidery thread.

Work from right to left on an edge or seam and begin by bringing the needle up from the underside of this edge or seam. Hold the thread or yarn down with your thumb and insert the needle at a point from the edge that is as long as you wish the stitches to be. Bring the needle back up through the fabric at the edge again. Draw the needle through and over the loop of thread to make a stitch.

Self-covered buttons

Covering buttons is a fantastic way of using up small scraps of fabric and turning them into something of value. It's also a fun thing to do with the children on a rainy day. I use these buttons for all sorts of decorative projects and love adding them to jackets and cardigans. Simply cut out a circle of fabric of a slightly larger diameter than the button. Place the front of the button centrally on the wrong side of the fabric and ease the fabric over the teeth on the inside of the button. Smooth out any creases and firmly press the flat metal plate into the inner rim. It should click into place with the button hook poking out in the middle.

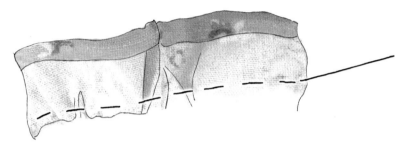

Ruffle

Add a fun touch to the edges of cushions, curtains, skirts and sleeves by attaching a ruffle. Save all your long strips of fabric and sew by either machine or hand. Simply double the length of the edge to which you want to attach the ruffle to work out how much fabric you need, so if you want to add a ruffle 50cm (19¾in) long you will need 1m (40in) of fabric. Hem one long edge, then on the opposite edge sew a long running stitch along the length of the fabric. Hold both ends of the thread and pull the running stitch so the fabric starts to gather up. Spend a bit of time evenly spacing the gathers and then attach to your project. You can hide the raw edge in the seam or simply place in the hem.

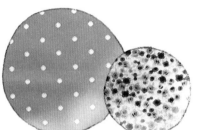
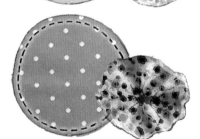
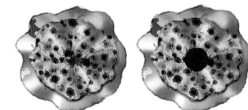

Flower Puff

I am addicted to making these and Beth had to stop me from adding them to every project! You can use them singularly or layer them up to create beautiful rosettes. You can also experiment with making different shaped petals by using the same technique but folding the circles in half. Cut a circle of fabric about 15cm (6in) in diameter and sew a long running stitch around the edge. Pull the thread so that the edges of the fabric are pulled in, creating a puff shape. Sew in place and use a button to hide the stitching in the centre.

Special thanks to:

Clarke & Clarke, in particular David, Sheila & Roy, Jenny, Rita & Alan, Dan & Emily, Andrew & Jules, Dean & Gemma, Sally & Matt, Becky & James, Linzi & Tony, Zoe & Steve, Andy & Sara, Jo, Ceris, Luke, Becky & Gemma @ Firefly, Becky F, Clare W, Katie, Cheryl, Barbara, Bill & Wendy, Ali & Barry, Helene, Cockington Court Craft Centre, Anita & Jared, Chris, Keith & Jodie, Auntie Helen, Claire, Emma V, Wendy, Ali, Coleen, Nicky, Catherine, Lisa R and The Mums of Collaton St Mary School, Lisa J, Claire and all of our friends ... for babysitting, good advice, coffee & cake, photo locations, props and continued support. Thank you all x

Project Design - Emma Curtis & Beth Parnell

Design & Layout - Beth Parnell

Illustration - Marcus Parnell

Photography - Marcus & Beth Parnell, Tony Platt

First published in Great Britain 2013 by Search Press Limited,
Wellwood, North Farm Road, Tunbridge Wells, Kent TN2 3DR

Original edition © 2012
World rights reserved by Christophorus Verlag GmbH, Freiburg/Germany
Original German title: *Brit-Chic at its Best*

ISBN: 978-1-84448-973-2

Publisher's Note

Abbygale is the brand name used by Creative Hobbies Group to market the authors' sewing kits and accessories. For more information on becoming a stockist visit: www.creativehobbiesgroup.com. In the UK, the authors use their own brand name, Hamble & Jemima. For more information, visit the authors' own website: www.hambleandjemima.co.uk.

Printed in China

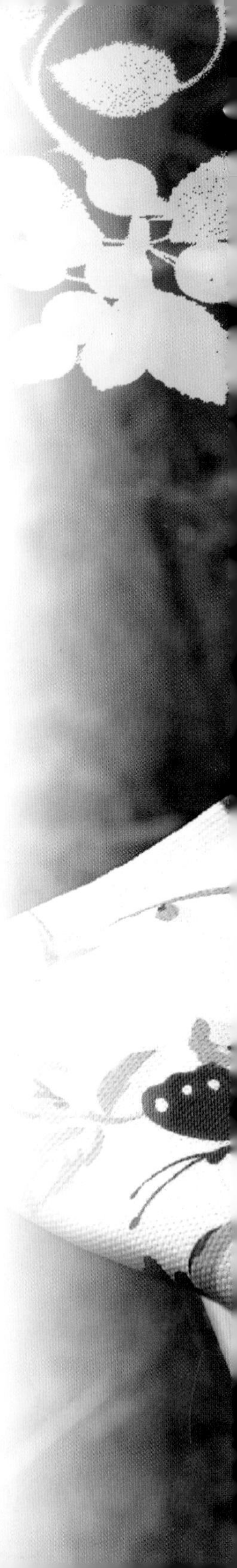